PRAIRIE SCHOONER BOOK PRIZE IN POETRY

EDITOR *Kwame Dawes*

CANNIBAL

Safiya Sinclair

UNIVERSITY OF NEBRASKA PRESS   *Lincoln and London*

Acknowledgments for the use of previously
published material appear on pages viii–ix, which
constitute an extension of the copyright page.

Excerpt from "America" is from *Collected Poems,*
1947–1980 by Allen Ginsberg, © 1956, 1959 by
Allen Ginsberg; and *Collected Poems, 1947–1997*
by Allen Ginsberg, © 2006 by the Allen Ginsberg
Trust. Used by permission of HarperCollins
Publishers and the Wylie Agency LLC.

Library of Congress Cataloging-in-Publication Data
Names: Sinclair, Safiya, author.
Title: Cannibal / Safiya Sinclair.
Description: Lincoln: University of Nebraska Press,
2016. | Series: Prairie Schooner Book Prize in Poetry
Identifiers: LCCN 2016007774
ISBN 9780803290631 (paperback: alk. paper)
ISBN 9780803295360 (epub)
ISBN 9780803295377 (mobi)
ISBN 9780803295384 (pdf)
Subjects: LCSH: Women—Identity—
Poetry. | Human body—Poetry. | BISAC:
POETRY / American / General. | POETRY
/ Caribbean & Latin American.
Classification: LCC PS3619.I56847
A6 2016 | DDC 811/.6—dc23
LC record available at https://lccn.loc.gov/2016007774

Set in Garamond Premier by Rachel Gould.
Designed by N. Putens.

Contents

II.

III.

IV.

V.

Acknowledgments

Many thanks to the editors of the following journals, in which these poems have appeared, sometimes in slightly different versions:

The Academy of American Poets Poem-a-Day, online feature: "Hands"

Atlas Review: "In the Event of the Last Unhappiness, Return to the Sea"

Bennington Review: "August in the Country of Another," "Autobiography"

Boston Review: "In Childhood, Certain Skies Refined My Seeing," "I Shall Account Myself a Happy Creatures," "Notes on the State of Virginia, III," "Portrait of Eve as the Anaconda"

Callaloo: "Doubt," "Incorrigible"

The Cincinnati Review: "After the Last Astronauts Had Left Us, I," "Pocomania"

Devil's Lake: "Notes on the State of Virginia, I," "Woman, Wound"

Ecotone: "Another White Christmas in Virginia"

Fawlt Magazine: "Kingdom-come"

Gettysburg Review: "Family Portrait"

Gulf Coast: "Fisherman's Daughter"

The Iowa Review: "How to Be an Interesting Woman: A Polite Guide for the Poetess"

The Journal: "Home," "Woman, 26, Remains Optimistic as Body Turns to Stone"

The Kenyon Review: "One Hundred Amazing Facts About the Negro, with Complete Proof, II," "One Hundred Amazing Facts About the Negro, with Complete Proof, III"

Mason's Road: "A Separation"

The Nation: "After the Last Astronauts Had Left Us, II (Laika)"

New England Review: "Good Hair"

Poetry: "The Art of Unselfing," "Center of the World," "Confessor"

Prairie Schooner: "Omen," "One Hundred Amazing Facts About the Negro, with Complete Proof, I," "Prayer Book for Vanishing," "White Apocrypha"

Sonora Review: "Dreaming in Foreign"

Tongue: A Journal of Writing & Art: "Spectre"

TriQuarterly: "Notes on the State of Virginia, II," "Notes on the State of Virginia, IV"

"Catacombs," "Chimera," "Mermaid," and "Osteology" first appeared in the poetry chapbook *Catacombs* (Argos Books, 2011).

"Portrait of Eve as the Anaconda" appears in the anthology *Bettering American Poetry 2015*.

Thank you to my mentors, friends, and muses for helping this book evolve to such full-blooded life.

My deepest gratitude to Rita Dove, Kwame Dawes, David St. John, Lisa Russ Spaar, Carol Muske-Dukes, Greg Orr, Susan McCabe, Paul Guest, Debra Nystrom, and Mark Wunderlich for all your invaluable encouragement, insight, and guidance. Thank you for all your help in bringing this book into the world, and for making me a better poet.

To Matthew Silva, my best and most patient reader, thank you for poring over every line, every word, each crazy hour; thank you for reading, re-reading, and always encouraging me to be my best.

Thank you to my sister poets Julia Cariño, Brianna Flavin, Lindsay Hill, and Ann-Margaret Lim for all the lyric beauty and inspiration. For all the laughter, thoughtful comments, and good advice, I am thankful to my peers: Shea Handa, Teresa Kim, Dexter Booth, Matt McFarland, Mirabella Mitchell, Becca Perea-Kane, Chelsey Weber-Smith, Liz Johnson, Callie Siskel, Doug Manuel, and Mary-Alice Daniel. To my friends Alex Carver and Allie Simmons thank you for all your support and for always cheering me on these many years.

Many thanks to Barbara Moriarty and Janalynn Bliss for always listening, and for all your reinforcements, especially when I needed it most. I am ever grateful for the support and encouragement of the programs at the University of Virginia and the University of Southern California, where I found the truest voice, the space, and the invaluable time to write.

Thank you to Wangechi Mutu for the beautiful, daring, and necessary artwork that peoples my dreams so wildly. Many thanks to Ashley Strosnider, *Prairie Schooner*, and the University of Nebraska Press for all your hard work and help in bringing this book to life. To Ishion Hutchinson and R. A. Villan-ueva, Don Share, Janet Silver, and the countless others who have encouraged and incited me in many ways big, small, or unknown to you, thank you so much for championing this work.

To my dearest friend Amanda Sullivan, I'm so incredibly grateful for a decade of love and unwavering support; thank you for showing up to my readings no matter where in the world they were.

For believing in the work from day one, thank you E. C. Belli, Liz Clark Wessel, Iris Cushing, and Argos Books.

To the poets who gave me the pen and a voice when I needed them most—Wayne Brown, Mervyn Morris, Eddie Baugh, and Derek Walcott—I am indebted to you for a lifetime of inspiration.

Most of all, thank you to my family for nurturing this dazzling life, and for being an unstoppable source of light.

The word "cannibal," the English variant of the Spanish word *canibal*, comes from the word *caribal*, a reference to the native Carib people in the West Indies, who Columbus thought ate human flesh and from whom the word "Caribbean" originated. By virtue of being *Caribbean*, all "West Indian" people are already, in a purely linguistic sense, born savage.

I.

Be not afeard. The isle is full of noises,
Sounds, and sweet airs, that give delight and hurt not.
Sometimes a thousand twangling instruments
Will hum about mine ears, and sometime voices.

CALIBAN, *The Tempest*

The hurricane does not roar in pentameters.

KAMAU BRATHWAITE, *History of the Voice*

HOME

Have I forgotten it—
wild conch-shell dialect,

black apostrophe curled
tight on my tongue?

Or how the Spanish built walls
of broken glass to keep me out

but the Doctor Bird kept chasing
and raking me in: This place

is your place, wreathed in red
Sargassum, ancient driftwood

nursed on the pensive sea.
The ramshackle altar I visited

often, packed full with fish-skull,
bright with lignum vitae plumes:

Father, I have asked so many miracles
of it. To be patient and forgiving,

to be remade for you in some
small wonder. And what a joy

to still believe in anything.
My diction now as straight

as my hair; that stranger we've
long stopped searching for.

But if somehow our half-sunken
hearts could answer, I would cup

my mouth in warm bowls
over the earth, and kiss the wet dirt

of home, taste Bogue-mud
and one long orange peel for skin.

I'd open my ear for sugar cane
and long stalks of gungo peas

to climb in. I'd swim the sea
still lapsing in a soldered frame,

the sea that again and again
calls out my name.

POCOMANIA

Father unbending father unbroken father
with the low-hanging belly, father I was cleaved from,
pressed into, cast and remolded, father I was forged
in the fire of your self. Ripped my veined skin, one eyelid,
father my black tangle of hair and teeth. Born yellowed
and wrinkled, father your jackfruit, foster my overripe flesh.
Father your first daughter now severed at the ankles, father
your black machete. I remember your slick smell, your sea-dark,
your rum-froth, wailed and smeared my wet jelly across
your cheek. Father forgive my impossible demands. I conjure you
in woven tam, Lion of Judah, Father your red, gold,
and green. Father a flag I am waving / father a flag I am burning.
Father skittering in on a boat of whale skeleton,
his body wrapped in white like an Orthodox priest. Father
and his nest of acolyte women, his beard-comber, his Primrose,
his Dahlia, his Nagasaki blossom. Mother and I were none of them.
Father washing me in eucalyptus, in garlic, in goldenseal.
Fathering my exorcism. Father the harsh brine of my sea.
Making sounds only the heart can feel. Father a burrowing
insect, his small incision. No bleat but a warm gurgle—
Daughter entering this world a host. Father your beached animal,
your lamentations in the sand. Mother her red bones come knocking.
Mother her red bones come knocking at the floorboards,
my mother knock-knocking at his skull when he dreams.
Scratching at your door, my dry rattle of Morse code:
Father *Let me in*. With the mash-mouth spirits who enter us,
father the split fibula where the marrow must rust—
Father the soft drum in my ear. Daughter unweeding
her familiar mischief. Mother jangling the ribcage: *I am here.*

IN CHILDHOOD, CERTAIN SKIES
REFINED MY SEEING

Sunset. That blood-orange hymn
combusting the year, nautilus chamber

of youth's obscurities, your empty room
for psalms, lost rituals. There find the bittersweetness

of one's unknown body, heliotropic:
Welcome, stranger of myself.

Consider the Jumbie bird clanging its deathshriek
like a gong, shooting through our mapless season,

unnaming the home you're always leaving,
scattering the names we have lost again.

The heart and its bombshell
bespeak the hurricane—

what has drowned, has drowned.
She will not return. The headless sky

unseals and aches for us, mother and sister
caught upon the steel hook of its memory.

Wet mouth of my future body, we've come to understand
each word, and how sometimes the words

themselves will do. Obeah-man, augured island,
I am called to remember the burning palm

and the broad refuge of the Poinciana tree.
Dear Family, how willingly I pushed my feet

into the hot coals of your lamentation.
Jamaica, if I wear your lunacy like a dark skin,

or lock this day away in the voodoo-garden
of our parting, know that I still mimic your wails,

knee-deep in beach, know I am gouging the stars
for any trace of ghost. For the algorithm

of uncertain history. The simple language
of our cannibal sea. If Grandfather,

your wandering fishermen still recast
their lives down on the disappearing shore,

know I too am scorching there.
Igniting and devouring

each abducted day.

FISHERMAN'S DAUGHTER

In this wet season my gone mother
climbs back again

and everything here smells gutted—
bloodtide, sea grapes in thick bloom,

our smashed plates and teacups. Dismantling
this grey shoreline for some kind of home, scared
orphans out bleating with the mongrels,
                    all of us starved

for something reclaimable. What chases them,
her barefoot rain, stains my unopened petunia, shined
church shoes, our black words, our hands.

I'll catch the day creep in, her dirt marking my father's
neck, oil-dreck steeped dark to every collar,
her tar this same fish odor I am washing.

I know I am one of them. The emptied:

How night comes raw, open-wounded,
her gills wafting in the iron's heat, sea's marrow
unrelenting, my heart one coiled mass

and sweating. I scald a ritual cleansing.
White poui tree of my youth
stripped bare, her burned hair,
what starched pleats of uniform.

My skin a red linen pressed through with salt.
The house. Even the body burns.
Carbolic disappearing; scrubbed pink into fingernail,
a prayer, bone of coral

scraped, kneaded
into breasts and thighs.
Frankincense and swallow a bar of soap.
But no washing will avail me
                    of this ghost.

I smell her at school and sulk my head
into the sand, watch my body carve
                    this resurrection—
its dull gleam of scales, a new ache:

For salt, for sea grapes, her brown flesh
sucked down like a thumb. Sun and snapper-eye
sucked out, her spine like a straw.

I cannot help myself.

Her keen and shadowing.
My hair still tied in her old handkerchief.
Pray, pray she is not here today.

Teacher, unbeliever. Chasing me home
to wash myself. Last week's daughter,

twelve years old, heart still for sale.

HANDS

Out here the surf rewrites our silences.
This smell of ocean may never leave me;
our humble life or the sea a dark page

I am trying to turn: Today my mother's words
sound final. And perhaps this is her first true thing.
Her hands have not been her hands

since she was twelve,
motherless and shucking whatever the sea
could offer, each day orphaned in the tide

of her own necessity—where the men-o-war
ballooned, wearing her face, her anchor of a heart
reaching, mooring for any blasted thing:

sea roach and black-haired kelp, jeweled perch
or a drop of pearl made with her smallest self,
her night-prayers a hushed word of thanks.

But out here the salt depths refuse tragedy.
This hand-me-down life burns sufficiently tragic—
here what was cannibal masters the colonial

curse, carved our own language of the macabre,
sucking on the thumb of our own disparity. Holding
her spliff in the wind, she probes and squalls,

trying to remember the face of her own mother,
our island, or some strange word she once found

amongst the filth of sailors whose beds she made,

whose shoes she shined, whose guns
she cleaned, while the white bullet of America
ricocheted in her brain. Still that face she can't recall

made her chew her fingernails, scratch the day down
to its blood, the rusty sunset of this wonder,
this smashed archipelago. Our wild sea grape kingdom

overrun, gold and belonging in all its glory
to no one. How being twelve-fingered she took her father's
fishing line to the deviation, and starved

of blood what grew savage and unwanted. Pulled
until they shriveled away, two hungry mouths
askance and blooming, reminding her

that she was still woman   always multiplying
as life's little nubs and dreams came bucking up
in her disjointed. How on the god-teeth

she cut this life, offered her hands and vessel
to be made wide, made purposeful,
her body opalescent with all our clamoring,

our bloodline of what once lived
and will live and live again.
In the sea's one voice she hears her answer.

Beneath her gravid belly
my gliding hull
a conger eel.

PORTRAIT OF EVE AS THE ANACONDA

I too am gathering the vulgarity
        of botany, the eye and its nuclei for mischief.

Of Man, redacted I came, am coming,
        fasting, starving carved

myself a selfish idol, its shell unsuitable. I, twice
        discarded, arrived thornside, and soon outgrew

his reptilian sheen. A fine specimen. Let me have it.
        Something inviolate; splayed in birdlime,

legs an exposed anemone, against jailbait August,
        its X-ray sky. This light a Gorgon-slick, polygamous

doom. And God again calling much too late, who
        aches to stick an ache in my unmentionable.

His Primal Plant remains elusive—
        Wildfire and pathogen, blood-knot of human

fleshed there in His beard. How I am hot for it.
        Call me murderess, a glowing engine

timed to blow. Watch it go with unjealousy, shadow.
        Let me have it. This maidenhead-primeval

schemes what ovule of cruel invention;
        the Venus-trap, the menses.

And how many ways to announce this guilt: whore's nest
        of ague, supernova, wild stigmata.

Womb. I boast a vogue sacrosanctum. Engorging
        shored pornographies, the cells' unruly

strain, rogue empire multiplying for a thousand virile
        thousand years; my wings pinned wide

in parthenogenesis, such miraculous display.

MERMAID

Caribbean thyme is ten times stronger than the English variety—just ask Miss Queenie and her royal navy, who couldn't yank a Jamaican weed from her rose-garden that didn't grow back thick, tenfold, and blackened with the furor of a violated man. The tepid American I sank with my old shoes over the jaws of the Atlantic could never understand the hard clamor of my laugh, why I furrowed rough at the brow, why I knew the hollow points of every bone. But dig where the soil is wet and plant the proud seed of your shame-tree; don't let them say it never grew. Roll the saltfish barrel down the hill, sending that battered thunder clanging at the seaside moon, jangled by her long earrings at our sea, ten times bluer than the bluest eye. That mint tea whistling in the Dutch pot is stronger than liquor, and takes six spoons of sugar, please—what can I say, my great-grandfather's blood was clotted thick with sugar cane and overproof rum; when he bled it trickled heavy like molasses, clotted black like phlegm in the throat. Every red ant from Negril to Frenchman's Cove came to burrow and suckle at his vein, where his leg was honeyed with a diabetic rot, and when he caught my grandmother in his wide fishing net, he served her up cold to his wild-eyed son: "Mermaid on the deck."

CATACOMBS

In the sour almond shade of the decades,
one last gull makes a long encircling screech
to wake the woman asleep in the sand.

The beach folds itself into the breath of each limb,
where her lone body has made a saddle of silence,
snuffing every lost call from the air.

Here, time has long stopped the heart like a stone;
the slow choke of asphalt, sweeping a bruised people,
drowned émigré of dreams, to the shattered archipelago,

the broken constellation of these West Indies.
There is no life beyond this quiet shore, but the toppled
colonnade of millennia, the last imperfections of God.

Black seaweed spawns like hair, lancing farther
into night, cutting through knees of mangroves
skirting their thick roots at the ocean mouth,

vast webs catching the debris of centuries—
the Spanish galleons wracked on pillars of coral
carved into weapons by the Caribbean Sea,

by that same foaming retribution which tore Port Royal
in half; its wrath uncorked to gulp Gomorrah down
into the volcanic depths of Bartlett Trench.

Here in the sand sleeps the lost chaos of a history;
she calls the ocean by its original name. The heavy apple

does not wake her. Beyond this white sea is only white sky,

the last black Anansi coiled tight inside the ear; beneath,
a vast hive of catacombs formed in the shape of a scar,
where the villagers came to bury themselves in sand;

miles of skeletons clutching each other from island
to island, linked like a shackle, femur to femur.

DREAMING IN FOREIGN

—after Caliban

Give your throat to everything,
not the word but the thing of it.
What the body speaks is untranslatable,
how always some unpeopled aching,
our mouths closed around the past
like knives.

Jah, mind our words,
our wound. Our runaway climbed deep
into these cockpit hills, kissed his good memory
into limestone, into blue fern-gully, built
that same fire combusting these stolen
margins, our scarred double gaze, shantytowns
slashed black from ear to ear.

Circumstance has made us strangers here,
wild dance we are slowly forgetting; what home.
The Mobay sky a lingering torch to mutiny. Rebellion.
Here I conspire with fish-monster, ignite and riot
with sugarcane, with shame-a-ladies, brush palms
in solidarity with each thorn, each shy tentacle,
our bodies opening and closing eager,
breathing the dark impossible.

How time holds me under
a shadow I cannot name, the bush-music and its sweet
bangarang. Do not wake me. Downtown
I'll roam wild with the improbable goats,
window-cleaners careening through traffic,

ripe urchin bartering his endless hope:
Each day is usable, I want to tell them.
Our hunger is criminal, faces sewn shut.

We are tongue-tied with the songs
of unknown birds, an extinct diction. Fireburn
that shipwreck, its aimless curse. Jah, guide
these words, this life an invisible column, my one
bloodline stretching, red livewire vein, to appear across
these hijacked decades, inventing Paradise.

FAMILY PORTRAIT

At our table we don't say grace.
We sit silent in the face of our questions,
a crown of mosquitos swarming our heads.

In this picture, some hot day in March,
the sun makes a strange halo around my ear,
light exploding in our dining room window.

Outside, the mongrels whine against our door,
two pups forbidden shelter for their impurity,
my weak heart dividing to offer all its scraps.

But what could I offer them, when I knew nothing
of love, and took my corrections with the belt
every evening? There in that city of exile, cobbled

square of salt-rust and rebellion, my father's face looms
its last obstruction, where the dark folds of bougainvillea
remain unclimbing; the one clipped flower

of my objection. That withering bloom still hangs limply
in its tangled brooch; my dress, my hands, bruised and falling
loosely about my thighs, unable to ask for a single thing.

And perhaps it was only the rain howling in my ear,
as I observe my doppelgänger in the shadows of the frame,
setting fire to the curtains while we slept. Poisoning

whatever dark potion fills my father's cup, my mother
at his shoulder with her fixed pitcher, pouring. She was

pregnant then, and still wore the mouth of her youth,

so quiet and unsure of itself, her fingers' twelve points
streaked across the jug's fogged glass. There I am again.
I am not myself—long before I shed my Medusa hair,

before anyone caught my sister eating black bits
of a millipede, shell and yellow fur snagged in her teeth,
I had my crooked guilt. My brother with his dagger

at my throat. This is us. This is all of us.
Before we knew this life would shatter, moving wild
and unwanted through the dark and the light.

I SHALL ACCOUNT MYSELF
A HAPPY CREATURESS

Our body antipodes. Brilliant lung and ten

good bones, crochet-neck umbilical, myself the yarn.

She carries her hands   her hair around like ghosts,

my nocturne-unfamiliar, coiled interruptus,

gooseflesh clouding our display case. Already twice myself
the noose.

No one has shattered that errant tooth, not even you.

The ocean sucks its salt appendage through my empty.

Already I have been a miracle, emerging

Still tending its incestuous wound.

And there goes our little world, set upon its haunches,
fraught with neglect—

Sister, we must eat.

Even the glittering oracle

of the bird-catcher spider offers nothing but the bones of bones.

Your carnivore unheaded   what stalks our puncturing

what marks   the mouth bewails its spaces, pines

for permission
to flush or anther.

Night prowls dangerous heavy.

Exhume a neon city. Our moon gone fat

With such astounding matter.

This feast parasitic.

Five days I watch its slow work with envy   cough up

beak and penumbra. While our one mind hardens its

                grief homicidal

till what inverts this lonesome dark I call thrall, luciferous.

                                    Mine only.

AUTOBIOGRAPHY

When I was a child
I counted the looper moths
caught in the dusty mesh
of our window screens.

Fed them slowly into the hot mouth
of a kerosene lamp, then watched
them pop and blacken soundlessly,
but could not look away.

I had known what it was to be nothing.
Bore the shamed blood-letter of my sex
like a banishment; wore the bruisemark
of my father's hands to school in silence.

And here I am, still at the old window
dying of thirst, watching my girlself asleep
with the candle flame alive in my ear,
little sister yelling *fire!*

OSTEOLOGY

Born four days late, a bruised almond
left puckering in the salty yolk,

the soft bone of my skull was concave,
a thumbprint in wax, like the coin

for the ferryman had been pressed there
overnight. When each of my hands glossed

over like a plastic glove, my pregnant aunt,
wearing a fresh bouquet of red hibiscus,

threw her body limp at the incubator,
clutching her own belly in fear.

With all of White House gathered around
to watch me die, they found themselves

instead marveling at the strange yellow
creature slicked in a bright shine

of plastic wrap. This was the first injury,
the one that set me in a dizzy furor—

a hermit crab scurrying through the sand
at a drunkard's jaunt, no palm cupped

wide enough to hold me. I burned often
at the candle, pulling fire through each eye,

consumed by the fever which beaked
at my limbs, *aegypti* mosquitoes needling

through my skin like air, each hole tattered
through to the vein, each sore left to suffer

at the nail. At the probing finger of the dark,
my grandmother's wet skirt casts a web across

the sea, pulling this borrowed body down
the tumbling basin, emptied underneath

the sand. All decade I've been buried, reaching
for a red calm underwater, drinking the same

dram of pennyroyal that washed her beyond
the penance of human suffering; waiting

for the black nail to shudder through
my heel, the last metatarsal sacrifice, the rust

of blood; lockjaw claiming every tooth
that drilled its way up through the gums—

hammered in on the cement, crumbled to chalk
against the bathroom wall. Nothing takes.

Not the brown knee wobbling dry at the root,
each keloid scar a notch for another year

survived; the parched ribs now emerging
as orbital rings in the mirror, famished

as the stab wounds left unseen, where every

tongue that made an attempt at the fighting

heart fed the countdown to this last collapse—
my pillar of bones with only dust left

to stand upon, this threadbare racehorse
finally taken down to the beach,

head buried in the shallow sea,
waiting to be shot.

AFTER THE LAST ASTRONAUTS HAD LEFT US, I

The ocean was at war with us.
There were men in space mending the void
between here and the falling stars.

My heart in their cross hairs,
our zinc roof unpeeled to show
toy soldiers cramped inside a matchbox,

tangled limbs melted by the great fire,
the Rasta man's lightning still crackling our brains.
Every time the thunder struck

my father bellowed out the name of his god
in reply, as we cowered in the damp ear of the night,
sucking at the finger-root of uncertainty.

I watched sea ducks, guarding their eggs like wet pearls,
lifted and sainted by the wind's fury. Saw my mother
learn to unlove my father, her bags packed

like a hermit crab, her white shell impenetrable.
My father, the wind, howling.
All the stray dogs had been scraped

from the mouth of the city, and we were one of them,
suckling for days at the bones of any animal
the ocean put in front of us.

Searching for my mother, the astronaut.
What flattened the azaleas I knew to be the voice-

box of God. And knew myself a black rag caught

in his dumb machine, made whole
by my fear, stories from Sunday school. What pulled apart
in her absence. America was at war in the desert.

I had seen whole cities turn to smoke through
a night-vision mirage, a millennia of history smeared
green like a video game. So my siblings and I crouched and waited

for their bombs, never forgetting we too were godless.
Back then we passed one sweaty dream back and forth
between us like a hot bowl. It could have been hope,

our heads two broken calabash halves,
catching the old voices like rain, while the stars held
their breath in the August shade for her return.

But one could be lost anywhere. Here in our sea village
the whole world swam drunk in the pool of my navel,
streets littered in emptiness after the last

astronauts had left us, my father one homeless lion
moaning silently under a broke-glass sky,
a blue palm bent in to feed us news of his storm,

the way what is unwritten whispers unto itself.

II.

O, wonder!
How many goodly creatures are there here!
How beauteous mankind is! O brave new world,
That has such people in't!

MIRANDA, *The Tempest*

NOTES ON THE STATE OF VIRGINIA, I

Child of the colonies. Carrying the swift waves of oceans inside of you. The wide dark of centuries, the whole world plunged down, sewn through the needle's eye, the old crow's glisten in your gullet. Eyes beetling through black. You wear your mother's face in the mirror. Your mouth closed around all those pills like teeth, each one so heavy your tongue falls numb. Think of your friend who only wanted you to find sleep, whose face asked you not to choose the worst. Dull wretch, slack-jaw orphan, you always feel sorry for yourself. And swallow each capsule like the last pearl your grandfather pressed into your palm. How he had dived three whole days for it. Your grandfather who loved you but could not say it. All the men who love you and cannot say it. Jamaica, old fur sticking to the roof of my mouth, the one long dream that holds me underwater, black centipede I still teethe on. Ruined train clattering through my track. Here, I could come up for air. Here, I could wake with a name I can answer to. Where Thomas Jefferson learnt how to belittle a thing. How to own it. He created the word and wanted my mouth to know it. He wanted the whole world pulled through me on a fishing string. Where I will find my fingers in the muscle of my throat, where I will marvel at the body asking to live.

AMERICA THE BEAUTIFUL

America this is quite serious.
America this is the impression I get from looking in the television set.
America is this correct?

ALLEN GINSBERG, "AMERICA"

Silent and small, his white-tipped quills
chilled this winter, a black groundhog emerges
from the margins. He wants nothing of the twelve white men

unfurling in their dark cloaks, each asking him a question
for which they've long chosen an answer.
A whole nation waits in front of them.

Like his fathers before him, he is a footnote on the year
like a hanging nail, no different than my wild branch of blackamoors,
cousins and uncles. My brother, dark and beautiful, marking

X's in his almanac. But the morning crowd, who must be drunk
this February, are swaddled in a year's worth of our island clothes,
Midwest-heavy with hope, or whatever drags them out of bed

to brandish signs, spit, and call, their worn breaths misting
each word's urgency, heart's compass frozen, directionless.
Who knows the dull rush of seasons here? The secrets of the finches?

Ask the women in the picturebox who now squeeze through
the thin mirror of Hollywood to swoon in Technicolor, lips
that crime-scene-red. Even the birds make gowns for them.

Slurping at their cocktails for the last scraps of pomegranate,
the wet privilege of their summers, their perfect skin only a Disney effect.
Camouflaged in witchgrass, small featherwork of children.

O to be hungry and to be in. My foot slips like a baby's
in this glass slipper of desire. While Phil dreams of hurricanes all winter,
his dark mind obscuring. The humans boo for a whole minute,

hurl obscenities at he who, quivering and illiterate, has done nothing
but survive in his pinebox and tried to understand his name.
But every night in America my brother is a criminal.

Gunned down for his clothes when he is not being shunned
for the shadow of his face. Even the weatherman is in a rage,
his blonde fringe frosting in the falling snow.

He is telling us of deer dying off in Montana
after their hooves have made a perfect spiral in the grass,
tufts of cotton caged in the thorn of each antler

stiff with the blood of too many of us. We have no words
for how we dream to die young. Dream to wake up one morning
and learn there will be an early spring.

But how many ways can we reinvent violence?
I hold this winter in my mouth like a pearl.

ANOTHER WHITE CHRISTMAS IN VIRGINIA

The house at the end of my street
has been looming all winter.

Perched garishly through this sour
season, pepper-lights slinking red,

gold in its wake, heralding the sign
of its own coronation, its million

chittering fires, Chevy-pickup colony
declaring the sidewalk. This their own

white sky, old names they refuse to bury.
The whole yard a boisterous spectacle.

I long to set fire to all of it. The glimmering
reindeer, fat snowman inflating his visible

lung, ghost child ringing his one hoarse
bell through the night. That bright harassment

of Santas. The idea of America burning
holes in the lawn. Who could live here?

With enough mirth to power my city,
enough of myself haunting me in some

other place. Nonetheless. One matchstick
man comes and goes on their horizon,

walking hard on his invisible horse,
Confederate buckle-stroke kicking,

toothpick silences. No words ever pass
between us as he hoists and pulleys

his large flag, daily hanging and freezing
through the verbless rubble of these

months, determined as an eagle. Clawing
at its steady rituals. *Don't tread on me.*

Still I am resolved to come friendly, built
and nested my cowboy greeting, torched it out

into this world and watched it choke
soundless, die with my good foot caught

in their blue hydrangeas. The hawk-wife watching.
Spies me smiling, waving in their driveway

of angels, swoops up her children
and says nothing, but retreats from

some darkening on the horizon,
some fast approaching plague.

ONE HUNDRED AMAZING FACTS ABOUT
THE NEGRO, WITH COMPLETE PROOF, I

In 1670, Virginia passed a law forbidding Negroes from buying white people.
This was 51 years after the Negro had arrived in chains. Free Negroes bought
white people in such numbers in Louisiana that the state made a similar law
in 1818.

Beware the African in his natural state.
His thoughts, much wilder and darker

than you can imagine, bisect in blood
knots in the trigger of his ribcage.

In the ripe season, his blood will burn hot;
each knot coils tight, a fist inside his body

with rigid animal violence, dark braids of hair.
Hope, an ache culled taut in his throat,

will strain to form a black bark of words. Do not
attempt to understand the diction of a Negro;

he wakes in strange tongues and speaks entirely
with his body. The Negro scrawls the language

of the birds, dreams of bold rivers and molten
crowns, your blue field peopled with bucksaw

and bur-heads, your hedges razed with pickaninny,
starved black-eyed Susans. Dark heads teeming,

remembering. Observe the teeth, astonishingly white,
as they struggle to gesture beyond anger.

The Negro will shatter before he is kind.
Their women too, like dark acanthus, bear

an unusual stench, are known to perish without
direct sunlight, and menstruate together. Too loud

and easily provoked, they horde in congregations
and spit from vast distances. All Negroes prefer

to be near the water. If they sense rain, they will swarm,
strip naked, hum, dive, demand to be reborn,

march barefoot through your garden to devour
your weeds, to spook and mark new heirs
with venom.

ONE HUNDRED AMAZING FACTS ABOUT THE NEGRO, WITH COMPLETE PROOF, II

> They could deal with the Negro as a symbol or a victim but had no sense of him as a man.
>
> JAMES BALDWIN, *The Fire Next Time*

Nature, we have spent our many lives
undressing,

our scowl colossal, half-light
stripped from eye and sockets,
that song bojangling, unrecognizable.

Home some brute sojourn
we wracked unspeakable, we mute vernacular
smashed nuclear sun and this code-switch.

All night the world bled on my fang
like a language and we unsmiling
                    our narrow gape
                    our space unslanging,

And all of us a zero.
Count old catalogues of bone, hair, teeth:

How broad how thick how beastly
and you the glass beaker of seeds
who gauge minute fractions of man, am I Orang-utan

Or am I savage? Neighbour,
I am naming you damned.

Blood brother, trained guerilla, renegade.
Killer. Threat of the Africanized bee.

Are we unsymmetry, skulls a million unfillable,
this dark uranium. With life half-cycling.

The parched chopper circling.
Cowed mammoth in the weeds.

Tag skin, brain, misdemeanour.
What was left to inherit?

Another spotlight
Nation, we are silencing
our many voice rehearsing

your shadow plays; a knock,
a hard knock, an illiterate dream.
O snuffed singularity—

How bright the searchlight
of our homecoming: Black comet
sprawling past black infinity, black heavens.
Black grenade.

ONE HUNDRED AMAZING FACTS ABOUT
THE NEGRO, WITH COMPLETE PROOF, III

Two centuries ago the Negroes of South Africa and the Northern Europeans
both practiced a form of cannibalism that was strikingly similar.

Woke ravenous. Woke with a mollusk mind

and swallowed all, you who skulked through
      the hull of me

and glowering. Glorious dead, I am inhabiting—

Sat fat in your feral sun mouth-wide

and purred with wonder, Hunger,

    small hands

devouring. Such darling flesh invents

the supple maw of me Moon-wholesome

and meager, what wet-nurse. Night's bivalve abandoned

and unhousing you. Meanwhile, in carnage.

Meanwhile in silence.

How all this year the mule season

Unbosoms me, my every throat
    a goring,
     that barbarous root

starved carnal, a plucked star. Sweet injury.

Drink plum-dark at the neck unhistoried,

avow its nakedness, your animal slaughter.

Slow massacre. Selves I am ingesting, what fodder.

Morsel, we mean to say. Wolf.   Bruise of unbecoming.

Imbibing stem and longtooth, wet seedcase, the butcherous fruit.

Reap tongue. Teeth. Skull. Genesis.

February, I am an open wound—woman discarded
and woman emerging. Scars devising scars.
To live here we know precisely how to be haunted.
Sundown sun, a sterile sky come running,
            sweet gallow-grass whistling. Ghosts.
All year we learn that chainsaw hymnal, outside the Lawn,
another excavation—slave quarters found concealed
in the student dorms; buried rooms choked, sounds
bricked off. Two centuries' thorns may break sudden bloom.
What can we say? No one speaks of it. I dream pristine.
And skirting the caution tape instead, we clasp hands
with each other in complicity.

Somewhere, the ghost arm of history
still throttling me. This taste of old blood on the wind,
the crouched statue of Sacajawea shrouded behind the pioneers.
Creature of unbelonging, un-name a new silence.
Magnolia explosion, its Leviathan shade.
            Then fall, what sick messiah. Fall, I am coughing
in the aisles again, where bare triage of voices pour
molasses in my ear. Where a bald insurrection of tongues.
Then squashed rebellion, scrutiny. Indoctrination.
To live here we know precisely how to be hunted.

WHITE APOCRYPHA

A choir of male voices
rises from a room
out of sight:

assured cathedral, bright
white jingle, their hymn
climbing and falling

for almost an hour,
cheerfully winding
and rewinding this way.

I've been waiting here
for a friend, hungry
and unpeeling some anemic

Western fruit, observing
in my hands its unnatural
rind, while their voices

break into dog howls,
all shine and no soul.
For them, the world is

lacquered and clean.
For them, every vibrato
is measured and paid for.

Even looking at the fall
leaves has its own upstate

vacation, and the old manger

is a catalogue photograph
where the wise men
and the moon are smiling.

I want that world.
Set in its wide white pearl,
unquestioning.

Who can say why
my sister, whose impossible voice
made the splintered

rafters tremble, and had women
fainting and bawling
in the aisles, could find notes

to breach that unnamable place
which filled and transfigured us,
but was not enough for her.

My sister, whose song
made me believe the soul
could bloom and flourish,

that God could sweat
and wail here in the mud with us,
still calls me weekly to say

there is no version of
herself that she can believe in.
Not even the singing.
Not even the song.

NOTES ON THE STATE OF VIRGINIA, III

—after W. E. B. Du Bois

Wild irises purpling my mouth each dawning—
                     trauma souring the quiet street.
Its whole dark field roots me down and down. The mock sun a blank obscuring.
Fire whips white-shock of lightning, bright Molotov angel, what ash marks
assume a coon cemetery.

And all the names scratched out.

                 What burns this house burns apishly.
                 The mouth the church this immaculate body,
such untouchable sounds we have made of ourselves. A blues archeology.
Thus like a snake I writhe upward, mottling and spine-thick, where heavy nouns
flay through my tubercular,

                 their heavens coil a twisted rope. Your veiled suffocation.
                 Unknown asphyxiate. The mourning dove which scales
                 its double gaze in tongues knows this: the broken world
                 was always broken.

How does it feel to be a problem? The mute centuries shatter in my ear.
                 The aimed black spear. This body, a crisis.
                 A riot. A racket. The whole world whistling.

Harass me a savage state, vast hectares will tar this noon infertile, each day a prisonhouse,
                 my sickbed caulking each bloom a bruise.
Quick hands swathe me in miles of cotton. Now blood-stained sheets in my room.

                 There is an old woman who is not my grandmother.
                 There is an old sadness I was born to wear like a dress.
                 She feeds me condensed milk through a bird-feeder
                               and smiles,
                 says don't pay attention to the flies in my eyes.

Love carved me in stained
glass like a new tattoo. Call me a curio, one Hottentot show. Ask
how I learnt to admire the prettiest bruise. Or how a body can
be sold into anything. O what soiled words I could fit my lips
around. And, body, found object whose hole can hold anything.
If I embrace this emptiness, all puppetry is possible. I stuffed
most of myself down his snow-globe exotica, found room for
my black head on his mahogany shelf. Squeezed between David
Foster Wallace and a gilded map of the Americas. He liked his
women unspoken, the body imperfect. To mark and remark that
terrible wound. No matter if sugar was dulled and unconscious.
He preferred to invent a person there. He ached to be inside,
thought he deserved to claim it; as if there was something here
to be reclaimed. Some mystery codified in the dark bone. As if
a self could be unowned.

ELOCUTION LESSONS WITH MS. SILVERSTONE

> You taught me language; and my profit on't
> Is, I know how to curse. The red plague rid you
> For learning me your language!
> CALIBAN, *The Tempest*

In high school boys were easy—
they saw none of you
or all of you

in one ravenous gaze,
slurped hankering glances
or walked right through

you in sterile absolution,
high-fived and hissed about
your dick-sucking lips.

Brewing names
for your body
in the mastabatorium.

Yours was an easy ripening,
this new narcissus, high-yellow
sparkle held fine like a jewel,

your one canary crowned
in amber, now hardening
a slow curiosity.

But the girls—blonde

and burning to a bitch-fever,
all suntanned limbs and tumid,

knew only how to hang
their barbs of laughter like a carcass
in the frangipani tree,

jaws unhinged
to a dark massacre,
fixed only on your studied disassembly.

Boobless and poor,
you are a faceless charity, a bloodshot
water lily. Stiff-as-a-board.

What self illuminable?
What sound among these selves

was plausible? Under their
shrapnel, your tongue heavy,
that girl too furred in dialect.

O wild naïveté.
How night unspools its vowels
in your unfillable

mouth inelegant,
and you the heir of nothing.
Such clueless heavens boast

their blind messengers:
French-kiss of catchphrases
by your favourite actress,

American gold
dripping honey
from her Cartier glitter.

Her language a white tusk,
what wild fire.

Whatever. Imposter.
Virgin falling through
your silence

your sky impaled, mouth
a crooked Valkyrie, unclaimed—

Study that diction.
Her holy existence.
Hot thumb

and revolver burning
the shape of an L, pink bullet for whatever
Loser was left.

Call this a triage
in your summer makeover, tell them
naturally your T's were the first to go.

Pretend what was pret-ty
only emerged "priddier."
Smear yourself golden

in their Vichy "wadder."
Somehow Mallory will negate you
in her arctic gaze:

As if. Fishlips.
Ugly in any syllable—

Let's call you mirage.
As if you were possible.
As if you could invent your place.

Rasta-girl, interloper. *Whatever.*

LITANY FOR CHARLOTTESVILLE

Heart—
long fogged with thunder,
let us spit fire through our teeth.

Let the long winter find us
sucking on charcoal, orphans
barking at a moon burnt out.

Let us be swept in the ear of an unquiet
morning, and remember the home
we have built for ourselves.

Remember this city's a blousy mistress,
her Sunday veil some pale American
whose brain coils thick with klonopin,

Camel Lights, and gin. Bless the ground
shook black with soot, the long strides
that carry you through doubt,

each night pulled up at the root,
far house in your memory blown down.
Bless the hurricane that comes for it,

as smoke clots to stone in some coward's
throat—O brute vessel stuffed through
with straw; the blond rust of autumn.

Eternal Father, devour these mountains
with flood, until what remains of the spirit

is purged, your old fictions snuffed out—

I am the wild diviner unparting
miracles this morning; may all your deeds
burn to nothing in my mouth.

In the cold pews of the chapel, Old Dominion, our damp
logwood misery is bare. Yes, we are nondenominational
here. Yesterday's rake is still hot on my back. And God, grey
huff of monoxide this insufficient morning, your white oak
forest keeps burning.

III.

'Ban, 'Ban, Ca-caliban
Has a new master: get a new man.
Freedom, hey-day!

CALIBAN, *The Tempest*

PRAYER BOOK FOR VANISHING

Anything black nuh good.

JAMAICAN PATOIS MAXIM

White mirror of morning,
the body is yours. Yours the face
to anoint with Epsom salts,

clean teaspoon of bleach
aside in the decanter.
What holy water.

Approach the angels
to efface this blackness,
another tar-baby, self

I am scorching. In the night
find nothing but a dagger of teeth.
Pitch-black marrow, vile

pigment unwanted,
set fire to my undesirable.
Un-soot and scrape,

until Grandmother, hissing
redbone made sacred
in her lightness,

liming me in talcum
before I faced anyone.
Grandmother, indelible.

I wear your undoing like a mask.
Wear your porcelain pock of dust
across my forehead

as one of the damned.
Sired in the image of no one.
Each day, each day. Accost the angels:

Marilyn, Jesus, and Mother Mary,
kissing their pink cheeks, the rail-thin
white skin of the heavenly.

Their eyes that same blue
swimming pool marked *No Locals Please*,
even now still glittering baptismal,

that clear awe in which I dived
for blessings, hid for hours
my kinky-head underwater,

to suck and marvel at the suntan taste
of foreign which could transform me
eventually. But Lord I think

my angels do not hear. Lord,
they are tourists gawking through
the cages of my poverty,

who take pity in this squalor
then return to far moons.
My black face

a blemish in their photographs.
Each morning the same horse-fly,

milk I must throw out.

The albino sun my enemy.
Whole days spent under cellophane,
under parasol, days wrapped

tight in scalding creams, skin a purge
of litanies. Baking soda. Peroxide. Blue cake soap.
Witch-doctor fixes for vanishing.

This ghost sarcophagus.
Come burn and beseeching. Come alabaster.
I drink and drink

to the dark disappearing.
That familiar sting.
The one sweet arc of my unmaking.

CONFESSOR

This is where you leave me.
Filling of old salt and ponderous,

what's left of your voice in the air.
Blue honeycreeper thrashed out

to a ragged wind, whole months
spent crawling this white beach

raked like a thumb, shucking, swallowing
the sea's benediction, pearled oxides.

Out here I am the body invented naked,
woman emerging from cold seas, herself

the raw eel-froth met beneath her tangles,
who must believe with all her puckering

holes. What wounds the Poinciana slits
forth, what must turn red eventually.

The talon-mouths undressing. The cling-cling
bird scratching its one message; the arm

you broke reset and broke again. Caribbean.
Sky a wound I am licking, until I am drawn new

as a lamb, helpless in the chicken wire of my sex.
I let every stranger in. Watch men change faces

with the rundown sun, count fires
in the loom holes of their pickups, lines of rot,

studying their scarred window-plagues,
nightshade my own throat closed tight

against a hard hand. Then all comes mute
in my glittering eye. All is knocked back,

slick hem-suck of the dark surf, ceramic
tiles approaching, the blur of a beard.

The white tusk of his ocean goring me.
This world unforgiving in its boundaries.

The day's owl and its omen
slipping a bright hook

into my cheek—

OMEN

Life has thrown my boxes
into the street: the good years,
men I wore like petticoats, sweet playthings.

The bright red dress of September now fitted
and filled by a new body. Young and hissing
like the croaking lizard that slinks in red-throated

through the burglar-bars at night, bold
in his stasis, laughing at me. Many nights
I have come with a boot or a broom,

often I have even mangled his tail.
And still the lizard returns, his old self
sloughed off, ghost a perfect paperweight.

My hands are the first to go—
the skin split dry and mottling, like
croton left to perish in too much sun,

its leaves unpeeling, its browned vessel
long forgotten in the yard. The teeth too
have begun to unsettle, egg-grey

and cracking here under stones, under bulbs
already dark with knowing that nothing grew,
that here nothing could take root.

Perhaps I too can be renewed,
mother and grandmother, one tail after another

I have snuffed out.

But the bone instead has chosen
to give way, while wild heliconias mark their shapes
in the hinges. Here, in this room and in the dark

of many other rooms, I make no sense of this silence,
how the corners fill and fill with weeds; nostrils
and ears overgrown, my one pink rose unpetaling.

The spotted lizard waits on my meagre life.
I watch and he watches, locked in one gaze,
his gold eye fixed, unafraid.

GOOD HAIR

> Only God, my dear,
> Could love you for yourself alone
> And not your yellow hair.
>
> W. B. YEATS, "FOR ANNE GREGORY"

Sister, there was nothing left for us.
Down here, this cast-off hour, we listened
but heard no voices in the shells. No beauty.

Our lives already tangled in the violence of our hair,
we learned to feel unwanted in the sea's blue gaze,
knowing even the blond lichen was considered lovely.

Not us, who combed and tamed ourselves at dawn,
cursing every brute animal in its windy mane—
God forbid all that good hair being grown to waste.

Barber, I can say a true thing or I can say nothing;
meet you in the canerows with my crooked English,
coins with strange faces stamped deep inside my palm,

ask to be remodeled with castaway hair, or dragged
by my scalp through your hot comb. The mirror takes
and the mirror takes. I've waded there and waited in vanity;

paid the toll to watch my wayward roots foam white,
drugstore formaldehyde burning through my skin.
For good hair I'd do anything. Pay the price of dignity,

send virgins in India to daily harvest; their miles

of glittering hair sold for thousands in the street.
Still we come to them yearly with our copper coins,

whole nights spent on our knees, our prayers whispered
ear to ear, hoping to wake with soft unfurling curls,
black waves parting strands of honey.

But how were we to know our poverty?
That our mother's good genes would only come to weeds,
that I would squander all her mulatta luck.

This nigger-hair my biggest malady.
So thick it holds a pencil up.

WOMAN, WOUND

Spackled yolk this morning.
The dawn a moth-plague
called down to winter.

Salt, old hair. Sweat.
Sprawled across the floor
in thick nets, body a slack

tangle. Newsflash of neon
in the windowpane—
Woman come undone.

Scales withering
in the heater hum, lips cracked
despite the pomegranate.

What myth. Sweet allegory ungifted.

What bitter vision tides the mouth.
The heart's shuttered stem,
blue-veined with drought.

December drinks itself to silence.
And even God in his thick brocade
has cast me out.

Frayed bosom taken out to trash.
Legs thrown to rust. The damp craw
of bougainvillea sewn shut.

Could I open wide
the sore uvula, browned with age,
to find the whole day used-up,

throat-white with wonderment
at what had passed? That he
was a reptile, vile enough,

scavenging at the gash—
but for a sticker with the shelf life
he offered cash. Black teeth,

black heart. Black vice.
Ruin comes at any price.
A livewire of birds, the whole sky

ripped out. Woman, wound,
dragging the star of archangels,
unwheels in midair, stoking

the white-hot clamorous oxides,
charging ions, charging
white bulls into spring.

WOMAN, 26, REMAINS OPTIMISTIC
AS BODY TURNS TO STONE

The fruits fall all December,
flesh pulled soft across each skull,
at dawn a feast for gingy-flies.

I mistake each thud for horses
out the window, where the sea grinds
the air thick with my mother's cannabis,

the pollen of her sweet cure-all,
as she collects the fallen mangoes
and chants my name at the battered sky:

Montego Bay, Thermopylae.
My finger a stiff bullet of karst limestone.
My mother's song her only version of prayer.

Little sister emerges from the wall to scrape
me clean. Dust settles in the fringe of her lashes,
but she does not complain.

All winter I've been petrifying in this greenery,
my body a fixed bolt; sheets of dermic ash,
stirrups of bone, and one black tooth pulsing

canines in my heart. Mother, your cannibal
lives there. Where the first teething
on rough cement left me dissolved

inside of you, absorbing everything

that made you ache—your clothes soaked
with blood every night, your hair growing

thick in places you had never seen.
Now this morning you have come to reclaim
me, carrying my name in your throat;

but I have purged myself empty
in our seaside home, a sea fished barren
by your father, his traps long salted dry,

the sternum of my body now a relic
in the sand, as grayscale claims this maw
of pelvis, my womb the coiled rock of coral.

Nothing will survive here.
Ossa, Infanta.

The world in bloom obscenely.
Pluming and dividing
while I crackle dry with plague.

HOW TO BE AN INTERESTING WOMAN:
A POLITE GUIDE FOR THE POETESS

Call me Mary. Call me Sophie.
Call me what you like.
I'll answer to any man who looks
at me right.

You may come to my garden
and steal hydrangeas in the night.
I'll suck your thumb
and play dumb.

I'll pretend I can make anything
grow. Rosebushes and violets
and bruises for show. I'll open
my hot mouth for an orchid

to snake out; I've been practising
this bee-sting pout. I will titter
and fluster and faint. Write hundreds
of sonnets in your name.

(Each one born fat and sunny.
Then I can claim to have made
something happy.)
Light pools slick in my eyelids—

I am all lashes and lips.
I have learnt how to smile, how to
talk with my hips, how to swallow
my words, how to make myself

small. I won't make a fuss.
I will coo. I will crawl.
And if you knock right,
this spine will give out—

I will crumble and weed and paw
at your feet. Unbraid and emote,
walk faceless from the brink;
if you spit, I will drink.

I will grow heavy and silent
and sick. I will strip you right down
to the bone. I will take your name.
I will take your home

and wake dark with a song
on which you finally choke;
my black hair furring thick
in the gawk of your throat.

BIRTHMARK, OR PURIFYING AT THE SINK

As you'll have heard, I'm no beginner.
The hand's thin muscle remembers
scrubbing the cloth this way,

three drops of bleach to the spot
of blood, washing away this little stain.
And cotton remembers the first month's

blood, how I brushed in panic at its scarlet
root, asking this blight to let go of me,
one girl branded woman overnight.

Each time I thought every man could tell—
us young girls shadowing each other,
making sure we hadn't soiled ourselves.

Face still hot with embarrassment
and what impurity we are made of,
whole selves being flushed away.

One whole girl whispering back to the snake.
Now three aspirin and mint tea are all
I have to my name. And the womb's

thick ache. Where my first child slid out
of me like a plum while I dreamt.
They do not tell you it can happen so easily,

just a mangled root of flesh and string.
That the blood in these clothes would be

all I have left; tiny birthmark

still burning red. Now I touch the bathwater
to my face, touch blood to my mouth,
wanting to drink anything left: Pulp, dregs.

Brute body. Heart, a black river branching
between us. Wound with nothing left
to answer for: Recall with your small mouth

all that I fed you in despair.
Wet stone, tea leaves,
our worn rag of silence,

half-mound of Venus fracturing
violet in the bathtub,

your halogen light
descending.

LITTLE RED PLUM

Crisis in the night.
My heart a little red plum
in my mouth. Glowing
its small fire in the dark.
How you, hand on my breast,
open my little animal cage
to watch me burn, eyes
marvelling at the birds
that rush out. My voice rising
red balloons in the air. My hands
find a bright cardinal bleeding
through your shirt, my name
spreading softly on your tongue.
Swift cherry vine galloping,
stitching warm skin to skin.
I reach for you, reach into
the feathers of the dark,
wanting to stay here, wanting
to press each hour into vellum
so tomorrow I may search
and find our little blossom
still unfurling there. I slip slowly
into your light, kiss my red
plum into your mouth.
Here. I give you all of me
in this little pink cup: hot mouthfuls
of fevergrass, of wild Jamaican
mint. Here, in the shadow of this
hothouse room, a red hibiscus
blooms and blooms.

CENTER OF THE WORLD

The meek inherit nothing.
God in his tattered coat
this morning, a quiet tongue

in my ear, begging for alms,
cold hands reaching up my skirt.
Little lamb, paupered flock,

bless my black tea with tears.
I have shorn your golden
fleece, worn vast spools

of white lace, glittering jacquard,
gilded fig leaves, jeweled dust
on my skin. Cornsilk hair

in my hems. I have milked
the stout beast of what you call America;
and wear your men across my chest

like furs. Stick-pin fox and snow-
blue chinchilla: They too came
to nibble at my door,

the soft pink tangles I trap
them in. Dear watchers in the shadows,
dear thick-thighed fiends. At ease,

please. Tell the hounds who undress
me with their eyes—I have nothing

to hide. I will spread myself

wide. Here, a flash of muscle. Here,
some blood in the hunt. Now the center
of the world: my incandescent cunt.

All hail the dark blooms of amaryllis
and the wild pink Damascus,
my sweet Aphrodite unfolding

in the kink. All hail hot jasmine
in the night; thick syrup
in your mouth, forked dagger

on my tongue. Legions at my heel.
Here at the world's red mecca,
kneel. Here Eden, here Bethlehem,

here in the cradle of Thebes,
a towering sphinx roams the garden,
her wet dawn devouring.

IV.

This thing of darkness I
Acknowledge mine.

PROSPERO, *The Tempest*

AFTER THE LAST ASTRONAUTS HAD LEFT US, II (LAIKA)

Yes, they had been brave in the face
of it. The Geiger counter

at navel-gazing.

Down here, Earth vespers nothing but its tinfoil
sermon. How to Survive These Extraordinary Days.

Particle angels   and lost radio stations
teach you how to read your self.

I sink like a pinprick through that Sunday hymnal,
and scour the worlds for proof of us.

Sputnik in the news. Mother in her vestal suit,
clutching the whimpering canine,

both of them orphans, inscrutable.
Stray

smiles emerging. Did I imagine it?
The moon between the pews, searching

for a tuppence, the milky congregation gone.
Her voice hanging its white frequency in my ear.
Gamma radiating

some kind of fractal   the dark growing older
between us. Each day mute

in its numbness.

We learned too well this steady decade of forgetting.
The wild   unfathering of it

Crackling her helmet static,
the same broadcast inevitable.

How to measure in obsoletes—
Ten cubits and a rope of hair.

        I press my face into the night and listen,
        mapping out judiciously the binary

of her language.

Some scarce dactylic.
Her song a distant banner.
Interstellar. Lunar. Monolithic.

SPECTRE

Invented a story, invented a girl
for you to talk to. Call me an easy animal
this dark season, a door for you to walk through.

I low my deer carcass slits to limbs
in your refrigerator, each pretty word a cigarette
you will put out in your skin.

Here each fault consumes the hoarding
of numb silences, the way you give voice
to nothing. Your hands still folded,

the phone unringing. A nothing hiss.
Nevertheless. I knell and touch mouths
with the mostly dead,

my self entombing itself.
The woman splits indefinitely.

                    *

My father spins his web of sensimilia
in the country, mother smiling
green in the ear of his god,

both teenagers budding new selves
in the cane fields. His voice is her voice,
their unlived life, my siblings and I

one in four chance to leave the slums

of this boyhood. The answer of his father
still unknown to him. But daughter

is always a sightless gamble. At night he dreams
of hands closing tight about her throat,
this poisoned root we must cast out.

Mother says nothing
and turns away, a worse
kind of violence.

Her good hair, her skin,
her bright hibiscus.
Her shoe thrown hard in solidarity.

*

I was born with one ankle
dangled in the sea, body grasping
for another horizon.

Hungry infant reaching for the salty night,
I ate leaves of scripture left open
to avert the spirits of the dead—

but already I was unruly and invited them in,
imbibed them in my fevered dreaming
until my skin was no longer my skin.

*

Now years later, I am blue October
caught in this southern gloom, thinking of
the man I have just welcomed inside me,

an eager creature still answering
the call of her body. Already he is
a spectre of some future patricide,

my long face in the mirror nothing
but the yellow smear of shame,
and he the same Western sky

I have been chasing, my country
nothing but a satisfied lover
now with no reason left to call,

the rain this morning nothing
but my father's spit at my back.

CHIMERA

Margaret, your phantom limbs ache
and marrow at my root, where we once twined low
in our dim husk of coconut, skirting the toxic drain

of milk, blubbering and hinged at the shattered
cliff of pelvis, reaching for the light. Two flies
drowned in the ink of absinthe, we slowly

ruptured at the liver, severed where the hasty
doctor wired her copper hook between us.
You were a fish caught in the clasp of oxygen;

your fragile lungs could not deliver you.
I clambered awake, sputtering in the night,
the worn breath of fingers against my throat,

imagining your plasma circling the basin,
flushed away among the day's last offal,
wracking my body in black contrition, wondering

why I survived. Mother, when she speaks
of you, does not call you by a name. She has
already abandoned your crippled stamen plowing

its helpless grief at the heart—but I was born
anemic and only half a self, purpling and diaphanous
at the wound, salvaged unwillingly from this divergent

sacrifice, still clinging to your absent warmth. Sometimes
I imagine nothing has changed—you rib and I claw,

sailing the earth in our wry husk, both preserved as one

taxidermic enigma, or coiled in a thick jar
of amnion in Mother's old cupboard,
dreaming the same dream in the dark.

HOW TO EXCISE A TUMOR

Don't fall in love with it, whatever you do.
Such affairs can only be temporary, and incapable
of feeling. Don't give in to its rosary; full, hot
breaths blossoming under your skin—it will always
want more than you can give. First entering
the mouth through sticky fever, soon its bald worm
will make a home in the damp chasms of your heart.
You'll begin to see the good in everything; a life
unwinding in cursive, your atoms coming apart.
At night it will move to leech at your nipples,
and other parts of you will grow hot.
Don't give in to accidental pleasure, seeing
the world in symmetry, or chasing after phantom
wants. This foreign organ will make good use
of its host. Blind aphid chewing straight through
the core. All day it will sleep and feed, sometimes
dragging its plump body across your floor,
lazily undoing your hair, and staining your sheets.
Making such a mess of your dreams. Learn
to turn away, say no. Skip meals. Abandon
your friends. Rummage through bowls of week-old
fruit, snipping at the tendrils where something
once grew. Imagine a hive of pearls coiled there
in the seeds. But who could ever live here,
you will wonder, old follicle split to nothing at the root—
even the once wilding promise of us is unblooming
even this sound for *stay* cannot be heard in a vacuum.

INCORRIGIBLE

All night I wrestled with it—
the onerous verse, trying to salt the wound;
there are worse things one could fix a gloom upon, I suppose.

But I fight to tack it down,
the indefinite I, I, iamb; to tease this venom out—
its cerasee vine grown thick as my hair,

pulling at my limbs, the fur of my mouth.
Opening my hand in the fissure of my throat,
a gutted fish, I am raking rut out.

Beached now on his shore,
blanched bone-white, I am watching my grandfather strangle
a bucket full of conger eels. Waist-deep in the sea's phlegm,

each finger a purposeful hook, today he is putting light out.
From the almond dusk, sun-roasted stiff, spinning
their brittle halves around, he offers each to me like an eager child,

until something in the eel's eye claps me shut—
dull movement I cannot comprehend. Need
to trawl some meaning from our grief;

to shake the vaguer shadows out—to rack the place
where something once moved. Suck the marrow out.
Pity the body who knows itself gone apart.

How shaking his rough hands gentle round my head,
Grandfather laughs like a loon, wolf-throated,

snapping this stasis like a nylon line. A frightened net

of sparrows comes loose in the air;
weaving through a thicket of sandflies, picking life out.
Are they watching us? Ourselves one drunk

sound in the soundless sea. Grandfather, dizzying.
Pity the owl-moth that struck with all its might,
night's shutters unopening. Moon at my window,

one slow eye, known-wound
I am salting as proof of existence. Pine this self amongst the green
Adirondacks, its blank hem of fog unfurling

where something else moves
in the eye's swift blink—beneath its greying leaves,
life's dark unstirring

flashed its incorrigible
scream of light.

AUGUST GHOST

My sweet grotesque
there is nothing left of you here.
Except the crawl of last week's
sporing; slow ferment of urges
you no longer feel.

Already you've reclaimed
your books (I did not notice),
have gone to build and nibble
at your worst obsessions,
still clinging to your last vice.

Now whole days and freight trains
pass between us.
Soon it will be rivers and mountains.
Soon it will be the half-buried sun
and the dreams I keep of no one.

At my gate the plumegrass still grabs
for you. But you peel them off
like leeches, and resign your absence
to the air, sneak in to snip at tendrils
you once claimed, to burn

what grew your body in the dark.
Friend, your name comes and goes
with the wind. Out west you will
make a mistress of the ocean,
ply the flesh of every orchard plum.

Be eyed and filled with a stranger
sky, while I shatter and rearrange
my empty cups. My long throat
still withering here with dust.

Perhaps one day you will ring
and I won't recognize your voice.
Just some August ghost
asking after fireflies.

A SEPARATION

Born in the ink of the vulture,
hauled beneath the same wing,
we were dropped like offal

across the waiting sand,
fingers webbed together
at the sinews.

There your matted hair,
your one grey tooth.
There the strange ocean

offered you nothing
but your fear of drowning.

How you crouched inside the palm
of a breadfruit leaf, sneezed black
feathers and cried all night,

already soured
to our half a life.

You wanted the breast and the bottle
and your thumb. You never learned
how to choose, so you never chose me.

Beneath the scar of our thunderstorm,
small bodies pressed navel to navel,
we resigned to suffer our two halves,

whole worlds existing between us.
Our silence. Our stomachs burning hot
in the Kingston sun.

Back then I wanted more of you
than you could give. Wanted to strike
you down with lightning,

and watch you struggle
with the sea. Will your hands
come shattering at my teeth,

or your hair, which never
stopped growing, come strangle me

in my bed. Where you found me embracing
another woman; the helix redacted.
The body unsexed.

I remember you spat
and this body unfeathered,

your tongue lodged with disgust
in my naked rattle.

Was it then I became something
you could no longer love, another
stranger you pass alone in the street?

One toothless bird shivering
soundless in the air.

Brother, I reached for you
and there was no one there.

IN THE EVENT OF THE LAST
UNHAPPINESS, RETURN TO THE SEA

I waited only a decade
for the package to arrive.

Wrapped in plain brown paper,
it came humble as a stone,

vested relic of my seaside home,
boxed plain as the last brown loaf

feeding flies in the window,
my mother a little girl hankering for it.

I was certain its whole held the cure
for all things. For my swollen lip,

for my yellow skin, for the wounds
I fingered open, for my father's sin.

For how badly I wanted to rib to nothing.
To be bursting and pregnant with everything.

Do not open was what it said.
(In the event of the last unhappiness, return to the sea.)

For years it brewed a dark hum from its edges,
and sometimes I thought it called out to me.

I hid it in my abdomen and tried to forget,
until the body found a way to flay

open itself, the way grief yanks its weeds
from hallowed brick, my family a hem

still unraveling. I awoke to find it hatched
like the cleanest egg, polished steel and glass

alive in my bed. The machine was small
and simple the way my life is small and simple:

only seeming, or aching for itself to unmatter,
to shatter at the heel of greater things.

AUGUST IN THE COUNTRY OF ANOTHER

Like any good heroine, she had nine ways
to bury him. Under the torn rags of winter
with the sea in its jowls, out with the icy
jacarandas, the fish nets blurred and swept

in the moon, by the tinder-music handed down
to her each century, its ballerina worn faceless,
arms outstretched, each day a faltering. A typewriter
ribbon pulled out, black fox vanishing

with all her good words. Then the lone cypress
groans blustering, untamed, its milksap grown thick,
grief prehistoric. What to do with the old summers
in the lake, what was found and renamed of each other

in the canals, each night a wild field of japonica flame
or what shook loose from her black river of hair.
What to do with all this sun, this lifetime that flared
godlike each August in the country of another,

and what cherished blossom pushes up, its old roots
and hands reaching. Today and today this one becoming.
The deer fossil the dog keeps uncovering in the yard.
The self and somehow the self still blooming like a mouth

torqued open in the rain, beloved and returning,
beloved and asking again to be filled, asking only
to be tended, to be bodied, asking what here
will scatter and what
again remain?

KINGDOM-COME

I.
The tongue finds the sparrow
softly nestled in the cheek;
a white call of feathers plumes
wild in each throat. Our murmurs,
pulled thin through the narrow

beak, coming to settle
inside the other.

Consider the gasp, teeth-caught,
consider this whistle through
the mind's thick chapel,
where you found me sounding
the warmest note.

Sire the muscle
bruise bone
make music of your brittle animal.

II.
I came to you hungry, and full
of dismissals. I came to you eager.

I came with mammy eye and pappy lie;
black duppy bruising you in the night

I gave you skin and bone,
I gave you teeth.

Stone after stone,
I swallowed anchor.

And nobody saved you,
white as a throat

as I washed Noah's animals
caterwauling from the dark.

Hand by hand. And shoe.
The water a black history.

Bathed them in a deluge
of the spit, the bile, the phlegm,

the offal we called lovemaking when,
eyes shut tight, you dared not look,

hands clasped for you a body
you would not see in the dark, praying

for your order,
for symmetry.

Well this sugarcane-blood was black
before the rambling sea learned

which names to call me
until I crumble like cornmeal pudding *Hallelujah*

and Kingdom-come.
Nobody warned you, cold as bone,

how this hair uproots antenna, red-ant stinger,
this kiss and this kiss a thick nettle.

No room on the boat for me.
No Bible passage.

No field guide to advise you to dress for fire,
to bring a thicker whip.

That what you thought was simple sparrow
was Jamaican grassquit.

THE ART OF UNSELFING

The mind's black kettle hisses its wild
exigencies at every turn: The hour before the coffee
                        and the hour after.

Penscratch of the gone morning, woman
a pitched hysteria watching the mad-ant scramble,
                        her small wants devouring.

Her binge and skin-thrall.
Her old selves being shuffled off into labyrinths,
                        this birdless sky a longing.

Her moth-mouth rabble unfacing these
touch-and-go months under winter, torn letters
                        under floorboards,

each fickle moon pecked through with doubt.
And one spoiled onion. Pale Cyclops
                        on her kitchen counter

now sprouting green missives,
some act of contrition; neighbor-god's vacuum
                        a loud rule thrown down.

Her mother now on the line saying *too much*.
This island is not a martyr. You tinker too much
                        with each gaunt memory, your youth

and its unweeding. Not everything blooms here
a private history—consider this immutable. Consider

our galloping sun, its life.

Your starved homesickness. The paper wasp kingdom
you set fire to, watched for days until it burnt a city in you.
            Until a family your hands could not save

became the hurricane. How love is still unrooting you.
And how to grow a new body—to let each word be the wild rain
            swallowed pure like an antidote.

Her mother at the airport saying don't come back.
Love your landlocked city. Money. Buy a coat.
            And even exile can be glamorous.

Some nights she calls across the deaf ocean to no one
in particular. No answer. Her heart's double-vault
            a muted hydra.

            This hour a purge

of its own unselfing.
            She must make a home of it.

DOUBT

I.
There's nothing of the dinosaurs in these bones—
no blue fern locked in the carbon fossil, spirals trilling
on spirals recoiling; question collapsing on itself.

Nothing carbon can claim to know of me;
three-hocked hydra pressed neat in my iron bone
binding these ragged and unlikely molecules,

echo clamming the garden dark as a bell,
thickening the Sunday crows like old London's
wretched rats, leaping and furring, giving birth
to themselves.

The sermon, if you please, is disease.

II.
Ring Gethsemane.
I shall be late.

Turning my hands
about some troubling verse,
my bald body stretched over

the silent ether, news of your illness,
your boundless assassins.

Still trying to pick a dim sound
out the clamorous tomb, a bronze chime
I can fix my brow upon.

But somewhere in Kingston
you are one with the mud,
lungs graveled in limestone,
mouth ajar, a jawbone still
begging the silent answer.

Only doubt unfurls
this wind of disquiet; my body
then too young and too unknowing,

now wanting,
only wanting to say yes.

III.
Too late at this hour to wean
the heart's wild membrane
still boomed against your flickering
memory. Against all my careful inventions

of love.
Blackness in.
Blackness out—

or something clever you might say
in the blue field where I dream you,

wide vectors of tyrannosaurus
locked with Nero's crumbled spine.
Where our whole beggaring rabble
is spinning to a blur,

all these vast oceans
still coming to a boil.

IV.
Find my body now at its empty page.
Blanched beyond the darkness.

Think a thumbprint of sand
in Eve's mitochondria.

Where I unburied my own shell
and found there no great design.
A plain bone
to be cast off

in a nameless storm;
these atoms flung wide and rebound
in the ocean's keening,

giving birth to my old selves
on a faceless shore.

V.

Another part of the island.

CALIBAN: Call me X. That would be best. Like a man without a name . . . a man whose name has been stolen.

AIMÉ CÉSAIRE, *Une Tempête*

CRANIA AMERICANA

The Caucasian skull is large and oval, with well-proportioned features. The nasal bones are arched, the chin full, the teeth vertical. This race is distinguished for the facility with which it attains the highest intellectual endowments.

Lusus Naturae
>>noun *(rare)*
>>A freak of nature.

Black body burns itself
>>to bushfire—
spurned husk that I am. Skinned viscous,
daughtering fever. Grief knifes its slow lava

through my fluorescent, gnarled
as if a neon viper, as if singed animus.
Gaslamp-hot for necking, lit oceanliners
>>>>gulped in.

Such is our ambush.   Spore of my peculiar—
Even the sea derails full-throttle at every turn.

What scurvy thrush unmoors   this boiled
microbial   as spite besots my humid mouth.

Storm, hag-seed and holy.
Come dusk, a rumbottle sky
>>>I am sipping.
My preening tongue, the guillotine.

Know nothing here will grow politely.
Such is our nature.
Such lurid rains sedate us villainous low:

This eel-eye screws to dazzling fright
   what slowly turns to vapor,
and another hot light spoils me
      for grotesquerie.

Sibling, Sisyphean. Howl of my unusual,
now we have reclassified the very
      ape of us.

Half fish   and Half monstrous.
Drowned spine of toothache take us
and barnacled, all crippled filaments
    all jawbone.

Already plucked   of cruder blooms,
brined hippocampus
    unzipped with germ.

My dropsied and unteachable.
Lo, this Indigene. Hissing into madness
this infrared. All night

our dark carousel haphazards,
   churning to house our many jargon,
masked congenital, and cloven in.

Diagram and mooncalfed. Even I.
How sometime I am wound with solitude.

   Enough a Negress all myself.

Scorn, one golliwog-bone knots the black
mock of me, naked and denouncing
   us artless.

Vexed skinfolk. Unfossiled, hence.
What a brittle world is   man.
Self inflammable, I abjure you.

And wear your gabble like a diadem,
this flecked crown of dictions,
                    this bioluminescence.

Predator coiled eager   at the edge
                    of these maps.

Master, Dare I

            unjungle it?

Notes

IN CHILDHOOD, CERTAIN SKIES REFINED MY SEEING

The title is taken from the first line of Arthur Rimbaud's poem "War," as translated by Robert Yates.

PORTRAIT OF EVE AS THE ANACONDA

The line "His Primal Plant remains elusive" is a sentence from "Goethe's Botany: Lessons of a Feminine Science," an essay by Lisbet Koerner that details Johann Goethe's botanical obsession with finding a "Primal Plant," which he believed was the "necessary and sufficient cause of all flora."

I SHALL ACCOUNT MYSELF A HAPPY CREATURESS

The title is a phrase from *The Description of a New World, Called the Blazing-World*, written by Margaret Cavendish, Duchess of Newcastle, published in 1666.

AUTOBIOGRAPHY

This poem is after Frank O'Hara's "Autobiographia Literaria" and loosely follows his form there, mirroring the first lines of his first and last stanzas.

NOTES ON THE STATE OF VIRGINIA, I

The "Notes on the State of Virginia" poems take their title from the Thomas Jefferson text of the same name. "Notes on the State of Virginia, I" references the invention of the word "belittle," which was first coined in the late eighteenth century by Jefferson in his *Notes on the State of Virginia*. Its original meaning was "to diminish in size, make small," according to the Oxford English Dictionary.

ONE HUNDRED AMAZING FACTS ABOUT THE NEGRO, WITH COMPLETE PROOF, I

The title "One Hundred Amazing Facts About the Negro, with Complete Proof" and the facts used in the epigraphs of the first and third poems of this series were taken from the J. A. Rogers book with the same title, *100 Amazing Facts About the Negro: With Complete Proof*, first published in 1934.

NOTES ON THE STATE OF VIRGINIA, III

This poem incorporates words and phrases from W. E. B. Du Bois's *The Souls of Black Folk*.

BIRTHMARK, OR PURIFYING AT THE SINK

This poem begins with the first line of C. P. Cavafy's poem "Sculptor of Tyana," translated by Edmund Keeley and Philip Sherrard.

CRANIA AMERICANA

Both the title and first epigraph reference the Samuel George Morton pseudo-scientific text of the same name, *Crania Americana; or, A Comparative View of the Skulls of Various Aboriginal Nations of North and South America: To Which Is Prefixed an Essay on the Varieties of the Human Species*, published in 1839, in which Morton proposes that the intellectual capacity (or lack thereof) in different races is based on the size of their skulls.

The definition of *lusus naturae* is taken from the Oxford English Dictionary.

"Crania Americana" also incorporates, alludes to, and repurposes the lines, words, and phrases from Shakespeare's *The Tempest* that are either spoken by Caliban or spoken in direct reference to Caliban.

IN THE PRAIRIE SCHOONER BOOK PRIZE IN POETRY SERIES

Cortney Davis, *Leopold's Maneuvers*

Rynn Williams, *Adonis Garage*

Kathleen Flenniken, *Famous*

Paul Guest, *Notes for My Body Double*

Mari L'Esperance, *The Darkened Temple*

Kara Candito, *Taste of Cherry*

Shane Book, *Ceiling of Sticks*

James Crews, *The Book of What Stays*

Susan Blackwell Ramsey, *A Mind Like This*

Orlando Ricardo Menes, *Fetish: Poems*

R. A. Villanueva, *Reliquaria*

Jennifer Perrine, *No Confession, No Mass*

Safiya Sinclair, *Cannibal*

To order or obtain more information on these or other University of Nebraska Press titles, visit nebraskapress.unl.edu.

CPSIA information can be obtained at www.ICGtesting.com
Printed in the USA
LVOW11s0023260816

501864LV00005B/397/P